LIFE STO[

What it is an[   ]

A guide for children and young people

Written by Shaila Shah and Hedi Argent

Photo: Gisele Wright

BAAF
ADOPTION
& FOSTERING

Acknowledgements

We would like to thank Phillida Sawbridge, Jenifer Lord, Marjorie Morrison, Ian Millar and Bridget Betts for their valuable comments on earlier drafts. We would also like to thank the following young people for their comments on the script: Sara Papamichael, Joanna Salmon and Shay Stuart. Thanks also to Zoë Harmar, who provided the illustrations.

Shaila Shah and **Hedi Argent**
January 2006

This book has been kindly supported by the
Stanley Smith General Charitable Trust

British Association for Adoption & Fostering (BAAF)
Skyline House
200 Union Street
London SE1 0LX
www.baaf.org.uk

Charity registration 275689

© BAAF 2006

British Library Cataloguing in Publication Data
A catalogue record for this book is available from the British Library

ISBN 1 903699 89 4

All photographs posed by models. Drawings by Zoë Harmar
Designed by Andrew Haig & Associates/Roger Harmar
Printed by the Lavenham Press

All rights reserved. Except as permitted under the Copyright, Designs and Patents Act 1988, this publication may not be reproduced, stored in a retrieval system, or transmitted in any form or by any means, without the prior written permission of the publishers.

BAAF is the leading UK-wide membership organisation for all those concerned with adoption, fostering and child care issues.

If you are reading this book or having it read aloud to you, it may be because you need to find out what life story work is, and what it will mean for you. Or perhaps you are already working on your own life story.

Before we go on, let's look at the three words – **life story work** – to see what they mean. The three words together do sound strange, don't they? It might be easier to find out what life story work means if we look at the three words separately.

LIFE	STORY	WORK

Let's start with **"LIFE"**. You've probably heard the word often and know what it means. The dictionary has lots of meanings for the word "life". We could say it is everything that happens between when a person is born and when a person dies. You can see it's a small word, but it has a big meaning.

Photo: Oliver Suckling   Photo: John Birdsall Photography

Now let's look at the word **"STORY"**. We all know what a story is from when we are very young. We could describe it as the telling of something that happens, either true or made up, long or short, with a beginning, a middle, and often an end – but some stories may go on and on like serials in comics and on TV. We read stories in books and magazines. We listen when somebody tells us a story and see films and TV programmes with stories in them. Everyone – and that means grown-ups too – likes stories.

The story of Robin Hood is a true one and has been told over and over again.

Harry Potter's story has already taken up six books and it isn't finished yet!

The story in *Eastenders* has been going on for years.

Dennis the Menace has a new adventure every week.

→ Do you have a favourite story that never seems to end?

You can write the name of it in the box below.

My favourite story that goes on and on is:

_____

_____

_____

And now let's look at the last word: **"WORK"**. You must have heard it often because grown-ups around you have talked about going to work, or coming back from work, or looking for work, and children have to do work at school. When we do something difficult we say: 'it's hard work'. We could describe work as something people do which is different from play. If you are asked to do something like clear up the dishes or make your bed, this would be doing work. For grown-ups, teaching, or nursing, or plumbing, or building, or going to the office, or being a police officer, or an airline pilot, or being the Prime Minister, is work, and they usually get paid for it.

Photo: istockphoto/geotrac   Photo: John Birdsall Photography   Photo: istockphoto/cgnznt144

3

Have you thought what kind of work you would like to do when you are grown up?

When I grow up I would like to be:

_____

_____

_____

Now that we have looked at the three words separately, let's join them together and see what they mean. If we join the first two words together – life and story – we get **"LIFE STORY"**. That's easy enough, because it means the story of someone's life.

If we join the three words together – life and story and work – we get **"LIFE STORY WORK"**. But what does the "work" part of it mean? It's not like the work the dinner lady at your school does, or the cashier in the shop, or the work you do when you help around the house. It's different, and it's special.

LIFE STORY WORK *is trying to put all the bits of your life – the good bits and the bad bits – together into one story.*

When children grow up in their birth family, their mums and dads, their uncles and aunties, and their grandparents remember their life stories for them. They may write down when babies have their first teeth, say their first words, and take their first steps. Or they may collect photos or even make a video or just tell family stories.

Photo: John Birdsall Photography

 They will say things like:

You and your laugh! Remember when we lost you in Woolworth's? We were frantic but then we heard you laugh. You couldn't mistake that laugh ever! And there you were, by the sweet counter, with a fistful of Smarties, pleased as punch.

Children who live away from their birth parents, and have had lots of moves and lived with different families, may not remember things about their life, or may be mixed up about what has happened to them. Sometimes they will ask questions like: 'what age was I when I had the chickenpox?' They will need help from grown-ups in collecting together the facts, their memories and their thoughts and feelings about them. And this is life story work.

Understanding our own life stories can make us proud of being who we are. Working to make a life story can seem like hard work at times, but it can also be fun. Or sometimes it can be sad. But even if it is, at least the work can help us to understand more.

→ **What do you remember from last week?**

_____

_____

_____

_____

_____

_____

→ **What is the first memory you have?**

_____

_____

_____

_____

_____

_____

Life stories

Everyone has a life story, and many life stories can be really interesting. You probably know bits about the life stories of your friends and people in your family. You might have read or heard about the life stories of famous people or seen them on television. Some stories are full of adventure and are exciting. Other stories can be happy when people's dreams come true. Still others can be sad, about people who have had difficult times, and they can even make you cry. Most lives are a mixture of sad and happy, boring and exciting. Whatever they are, they make a good story, and everyone loves a good story!

Many people like reading real life stories in books. If you write your own book about yourself, it is called an "autobiography". When another person writes about you, it is called a "biography". These are just more words for life stories that could be about famous people – leaders of countries, film stars, people who have invented things, people who have discovered different parts of the world, kings and queens, and people who have led special lives.

In the box below, write down the names of three famous life stories you know.

_____

_____

_____

Here are some life stories that you might have heard about. David Beckham is a famous footballer, and the captain of the England team. Princess Diana was married to Prince Charles, and sadly died many years ago. She loved children, and Prince William and Prince Harry are her sons. Nelson Mandela is a famous leader in South Africa and was in prison for many years. When he came out, he became President Mandela.

You may also have heard about John Lennon, one of the Beatles, or Helen Keller, who was born deaf and dumb but became a famous teacher and writer. Or about Muhammad Ali, a boxer, who was also a champion of black Americans. Or you may have learnt at school about Queen Victoria, or King Charles who had his head cut off, or Henry VIII who had six wives, or Captain Scott, who went to the South Pole, or Christopher Columbus, who sailed round the world, or Florence Nightingale or Mary Seacole, both brave nurses in a war long ago.

Henry VIII

Photo: National Portrait Gallery, London

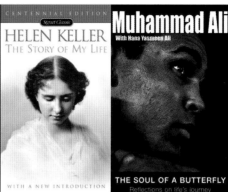

CENTENNIAL EDITION

Signet Classic

HELEN KELLER
THE STORY OF MY LIFE

WITH A NEW INTRODUCTION

Muhammad Ali
With Hana Yasmeen Ali

THE SOUL OF A BUTTERFLY
Reflections on life's journey

Captain Scott   Mary Seacole

Photo: National Portrait Gallery, London   Photo: © Courtesy Helen Rappaport/
National Portrait Gallery, London

A diary is yet another way of writing about your life and what happens to you. Have you ever kept a diary?

_____

_____

_____

Or do you know anyone else who keeps a diary?

_____

_____

_____

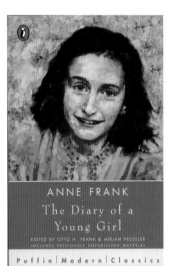

ANNE FRANK
The Diary of a
Young Girl
EDITED BY OTTO H. FRANK & MIRJAM PRESSLER
INCLUDES PREVIOUSLY UNPUBLISHED MATERIAL

Puffin|Modern|Classics

If you write down regularly what you have done, or thought, or felt, it will remind you of good times as well as hard times later. Anne Frank wrote a diary when she was hiding from the German army. Now we can all read her story to help us understand what happened to her and her family. Anne Frank wrote her diary in a special book she had been given for her 12th birthday. It even had a lock and key. But you can also use an ordinary exercise book as long as you put the date each time you write in it.

Martina had a "treasure box" – an old biscuit tin in which she kept all her most precious belongings. In it, she kept a tiny rag doll from when she was a baby, a photo of her Mum and little sister, her first tooth that came out the day she started school, a programme from

Photo: Roger Harmar

Disneyland, a blue sparkly ribbon, two shells and a scrapbook from her best holiday in Wales, a football made of marzipan from her last birthday cake, when she was eight, a copy of her birth certificate, a train ticket to London, and a little book with the names and addresses of all the people she specially liked.

So you see, stories can be told in different ways. You can write them down in a book or keep a diary. Or you can make a film or a play out of a story. Or you can put together different things like letters and cards and photographs and anything else that reminds you of your life so far. You may even have your own special collection to help you to remember, like Martina.

The important thing is, of course, that your life story is about **YOU**.

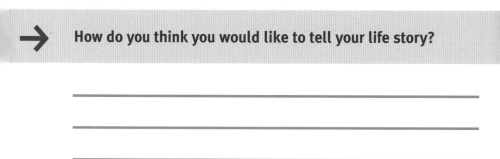

→ **How do you think you would like to tell your life story?**

Everyone's story is important to them. Everyone needs to know why they are where they are and what happened to them along the way. That's why people sometimes call it a life journey.

⊙ Why your life story is important

If you have been separated from your birth family, and have lived with different foster families and moved around a lot, what happened to you could be muddling. You will want to understand why you are not living with your birth parents, and why you are where you are today. You will want to make sure that you don't lose any part of your own story and that you can take it with you wherever you go. Your life story is one of those unending stories that will go on and on for as long as you live! Whenever you put it together and however you do it, you will be doing LIFE STORY WORK and most likely you will be making some kind of a **life story book**.

→ **Why do you think your life story is important?**

_____

_____

_____

⊙ When do you make a life story book?

If you have a social worker, she or he will most probably suggest that you start a life story book while you are living with a foster family, or with other children in a children's home, so that you remember the important things that have happened to you so far. Often children make a life story book when they are getting ready to move again, or if they are going to be adopted or when they have already been adopted. Most children work on their life stories maybe once or twice a week, after school or at the weekend.

Sam is seven years old. He has lived with his foster carers since he was four, and now he is going to be adopted by another family. Sam sees his birth mother sometimes, and his gran, but not his birth father. All his memories of when he was little are a bit muddled up. He wants to be adopted, but he doesn't want to lose his birth mother and his foster family. Sam's social worker is helping him to make a book with

pictures and photos and writing. She meets him every Tuesday and first they have a drink and talk. Then they work on the life story book. Afterwards, Sam always chooses a game they can play together.

Photo: Gary Brown

◎ Who can help to make a life story book?

Your social worker and the people you are living with will help you. They will buy you all the stuff you need and make sure that you have a quiet place to work in. They will help you to collect the information and everything else you want to put in the book, and they will help you to write in it or they will write for you. Your birth family may also be able to help by finding photographs and telling family stories you don't remember.

Sam's grandma looked after him until he was fostered. Sam and his social worker visit Gran and she gives them lots of family snaps for Sam's book, and tells them stories about when Sam was a baby. On the way back to the foster home, they drive past the hospital where Sam was born, and they take a photo of it to stick in the book.

Photo: Gary Brown

What do you need to make a life story book?

All you need to begin with is paper for writing, drawing, painting and sticking pictures on, and a safe box to keep everything you collect and want to use. Some children choose to work with large sheets of paper and some prefer to have a proper book with blank pages. One little boy decided to put his life story on a roll of white wallpaper, so that he could always start by looking at where he had got to, and then unroll it right back to the day he was born. If you don't want to make your very own book, it is possible to buy a ready-made life story book called *My Life and Me*, which you can fill in with your own story (see page 29).

You will also want to have good crayons and felt tip pens, scissors, glue, paints if you enjoy painting, glitter maybe, and a set of your favourite stickers to decorate your work.

Your life story is precious, so always put it in a safe place when you are not working on it, or ask your foster carer to look after it for you.

My life
and me

paste a picture
of yourself here

by

What goes in a life story book?

Have you ever heard the saying *"anything goes"*? Well, anything can go into your life story book as long as it's what you want. It's going to be YOUR story, so you should tell the people helping you what goes in and what stays out.

Sam wanted a photo of his mum and gran and of the foster carers with their dog in his book, but he didn't want to have a picture of his dad. Instead, he asked his social worker to write: 'I don't want to see my dad because he hurt me and makes me sad

Photo: Gary Brown

and I don't want his photo in my book'. Of course, Sam did put in lots of pictures of himself!

 Can you think of something you don't want to put in your book?

_____

_____

_____

_____

_____

You could cut out pictures from magazines, like Ruby, who wanted to include her favourite pop groups, or like Leo, who stuck in pictures of butterflies because he was so interested in them.

Some children like to put in certificates for swimming or road safety, or good school attendance or sports events or music grades. Lorraine went to a city farm and won a rosette for horse riding, which she glued to the front of her book. And underneath she wrote: '*I won this rosette when I was nine for riding on a pony called "Merrylegs". I loved Merrylegs very much and I want to go riding again.*'

Bus and train tickets, or programmes, or post cards, or something out of a cracker, or even a chocolate wrapper, could remind you of a special day. Maps and diagrams and your own drawings of what you remember, can show who you are and where you have come from.

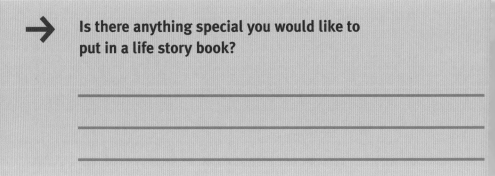

→ **Is there anything special you would like to put in a life story book?**

_____

_____

_____

◉ ## Who does the life story book belong to?

Life story books belong to the children who make them. If you are making a book, it will always belong to you and you will be able to take it with you wherever you go and show it to people you choose. Some children take their books to school, so that their teachers can see all the work they have done.

Because it is an unending story, it is important to look after your book if you have one. You will want to add to it as you grow older, and you will want to look at it many times and you may want to share it with other people.

Sam wants to take his book with him when he meets his new parents so that they will know all about him and about the people who are important to him.

Do I have to make a life story book?

No. You don't have to make a book. You can tell your story in a different way like the boy who used a roll of wallpaper, or you can use a shoebox or a folder to keep everything in. Or you can just talk to someone about what you remember and how you feel about it and ask for help to fill in the gaps.

If you know how to use the computer, you can use a CD called *My Life Story* (see page 30). It has pictures and games, and is set on a treasure island! It lets you put together information about yourself and is good fun to use. Sometimes children like to tell their stories using puppets or while they play with a doll's house or a train set. That's all life story work. Making a book is just one way of putting the story together and keeping it safe.

Photo: Bonnie Jacobs

My Life Story

Rina didn't want to make a book, or to have a box to keep things in or to do anything else her social worker suggested. But Rina loved maps and she drew a huge map to show all the houses she had lived in and the long and short roads in between. She drew all the people who lived in the houses and she wrote their names underneath. Then she decided to stick a golden star on the places and people she liked and a red spot on the places and people that had made her unhappy. It was a very good piece of life story work, and Rina's foster carer helped her to mount the map on cardboard and hang it up on her bedroom wall.

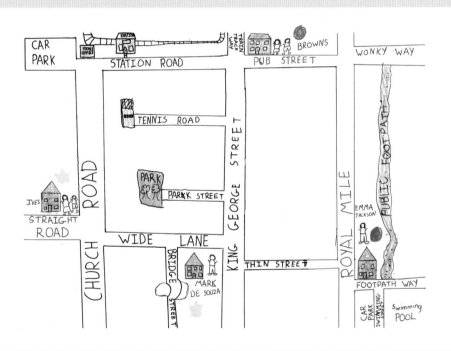

More tips for life story work

1 Make a family tree

Children who are adopted or live with foster carers, sometimes find it difficult to know exactly where they belong. But you will always be part of your birth family. Ask your social worker, or your foster carer or your parents or your teacher to help you draw a diagram, something like this:

My birth family

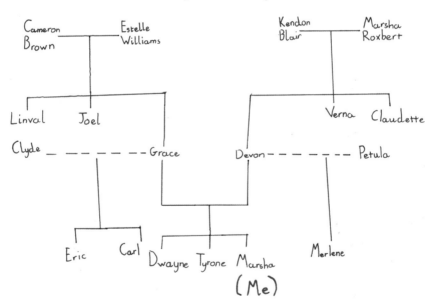

This kind of diagram is sometimes called a **"genogram"**.

Or you can draw a real tree and place all your birth family on the branches on one side, and your foster family or adoptive family on the branches on the other side. Then put yourself at the very top of the tree in the middle, something like this:

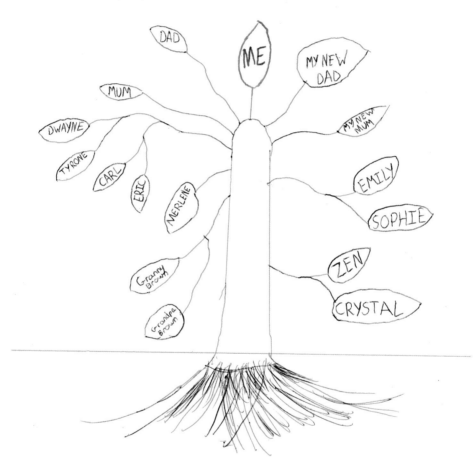

Can you see how strong the roots are? Don't forget to draw the roots on your tree so that it can grow.

2 Think about family circles

All the people who make up a family belong to a family circle. When anyone marries or leaves home or if children are fostered or adopted, they become part of another family circle as well.

 How many family circles do you belong to?

If you belong to more than one family circle, you can draw them to overlap something like this:

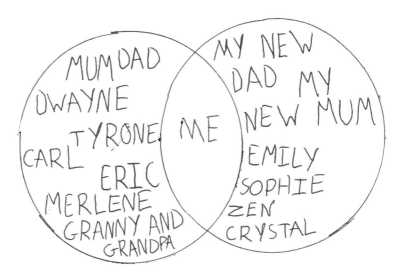

Can you see how you can belong to both circles at the same time?

Here is another way of working with circles:

Ella drew a small circle and in it she wrote the names of the people she really loved: Mum, Dad, Grandpa, brother John, and her foster carers and their baby and their dog. Then she drew a larger circle around the small one and in that she wrote the names of people she liked a lot: her best friend, her teacher, her social worker, her first foster carers, the local doctor, her auntie and uncle and all her cousins. Finally, she drew a very big circle around the other two, and in the outside ring she listed the other people she cared about: the lady in the library, the man in the corner shop, the postman who brings her letters from her brother, five more children from her class, and the neighbours from where she used to live.

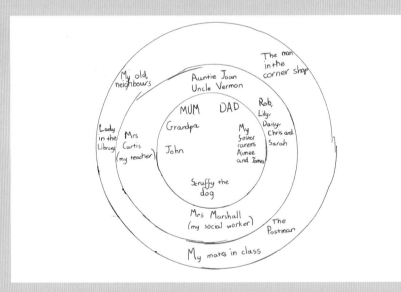

Ella will always remember the important people in her life because the circles keep them all together and they show how she feels about them.

3 Imagine a journey

There are many ways of showing where you have come from, how you have travelled, and where you are going. Rina made a map – do you remember? You could pretend you're a train and draw a railway line with stations to mark where you have stopped and signposts showing where you are heading for.

Or perhaps you could have a winding path or river with all the places you have lived in and the people you want to remember on either side. You can put in flowers or stars for happy feelings and clouds and rain for when you were sad.

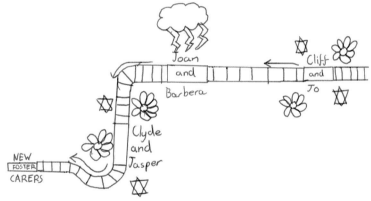

→ **Can you think of another way to describe a journey?**

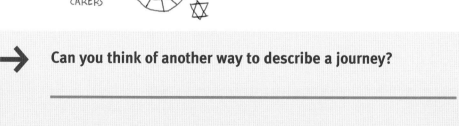

How about a flight of stairs?
A boy called Khalil made a model of a flight of steps. He said every stair was like a step in his life and he wrote on each stair about what had happened to him. Khalil had come from another country and his journey had been lonely and hard. Now he hoped the stairs would lead him up to a better life.

4 Getting to know your new family

It's important for new families and children to get to know each other. One way of doing that is to make a list of everything you will want to know about a new family. You can ask your social worker or carer to help you. Sam made this list for his new family.

Do you live near the seaside?
Do you have children?
Are you very strict?
Do you watch Top of the Pops?
How old are you?
Will you get cross with me?
Can I have a bike?

Sam asked lots more questions.

→ **What questions would you like to ask?**

_____

_____

_____

You can then make a list of everything you will want a family to know about **YOU**. This is Sam's list.

I'm shy when I meet people
Sometimes I feel sad and I don't know why
I giggle a lot
I want to have a best friend
I don't know if I'll like school
I hate vegetables
I can't read very well

Sam said lots more about himself.

What would you like to say about yourself?

_____

_____

_____

_____

_____

_____

_____

_____

_____

Don't forget, you are putting YOUR life story together and you can say or write or draw or stick in, or keep out, anything at all, because "anything goes" in life story work.

Good luck! Enjoy your life story work!
And be proud of your story.

My Life and Me, Jean Camis

Durable and comprehensive, this life story book can be used flexibly by any child. Colour-coded sections include space for drawings, photographs, documents and a record of feelings and thoughts at various stages in the child's life. Practice guidelines will help those undertaking direct work with the child.

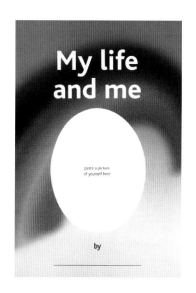

BAAF 2001
A4, 121 page plus guidelines
£13.62 plus VAT (£2.38)
£16.00 total

My Life Story CD-ROM, Bridget Betts and Afshan Ahmad

My Life Story is a children's resource designed as an interactive CD-ROM. It aims to guide worker and child through a range of activities to assemble key information, process current situations and consider what the future might hold. It has seven interactive sections with a wide range of activities, user input, printable worksheets and help. Music, sound, colour animation, attractive graphics and interactivity ensure that it is as much fun as it is useful.
Information Plus 2003
£59.53 plus VAT (£10.42) **£69.95 total**

Life Story Work, Tony Ryan and Rodger Walker

Life Story Work is an authoritative guide that will help anyone who wants to use life story work as a way of helping children. The authors, both experienced practitioners, present a rich and creative assortment of useful techniques and exercises for adults working with children – social workers, adoptive parents, foster carers, residential staff, teachers and nursery workers.
BAAF 1999, A4, 70 pages, **£12.95**

These three resources are available from BAAF Publications, Skyline House, 200 Union Street, London SE1 0LX.

Please see **www.baaf.org.uk** for the full catalogue of BAAF titles.